Seeing Things Differently

Philip D. Zimmerman

A Winterthur Book

Winterthur, Delaware

This book was made possible through a grant
from the Chipstone Foundation and the many
contributors to the campaign for Winterthur

Seeing Things Differently accompanies a permanent
exhibition entitled "Perspectives on the
Decorative Arts in Early America," which opened
in the Winterthur Galleries October 1992.
The planning and implementation of this exhibition
was funded in part by grants from the
National Endowment for the Humanities.

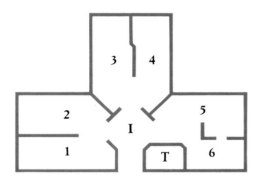

I – Introduction
1 – Change over Place
2 – Change over Time
3 – Techniques and Technology
4 – Maker and Marketplace
5 – Ritual and Custom
6 – Messages and Symbols
T – Theater

Acknowledgements

In today's world of detailed technical information, subject specialization, and diverse interests and points of view, presentation of broadly conceived topics is beyond the capabilities of a single author. *Seeing Things Differently* is no exception. From its inception, this publication was the product of many forums in which ideas were freely expressed and sometimes ardently defended.

At the core of these efforts was a team of Winterthur colleagues charged with developing a permanent exhibition for a new gallery facility. Two years of discussions shaped the material presented here, and I acknowledge with gratitude my indebtedness to each member of the team. Team members included Albert P. Albano, Jennifer Anderson-Lawrence, Peter Hammell, Amanda E. Lange, Susan B. Swan, and Robert F. Trent. I owe special thanks to team members Pauline K. Eversmann, Donald L. Fennimore, Jr., Caitlin McQuade, and Karol A. Schmiegel for their helpful comments on the text. Kenneth L. Ames was instrumental in shaping the direction of the exhibition story line, as was E. McSherry Fowble who reviewed drafts and helped with many particularly nettlesome areas.

Marian T. Clowes, Charles F. Hummel, and Pamela H. Simpson, a visiting scholar from Washington and Lee University, read the manuscript and offered sensitive comments and suggestions.

With great pleasure I also acknowledge the substantial contributions of Richard M. Candee, Barbara Clark Smith, Grant McCracken, Dennis O'Toole, and Patterson B. Williams, project consultants to the new exhibition under a planning grant from the National Endowment for the Humanities.

Catherine E. Hutchins, acting director of Winterthur's publications division, envisioned the final product, providing her always balanced and expert editorial advice and, with the help of Susan Randolph, guided it to completion. Winterthur's conservators examined and treated the objects in anticipation of photography. George J. Fistrovich provided photography that is the next best thing to seeing the objects and, in a few instances, arguably better.

Finally, publication funds were supplied in part by a generous grant from the Chipstone Foundation, Milwaukee. Remaining funds were provided by the hundreds of donors to Winterthur's $19.5 million capital campaign, a fundraising venture that has enhanced the museum's ability to present its extraordinary collection to new audiences in new ways.

Director's Statement

Since 1951 Winterthur has actively pursued four objectives that are at the heart of most museums—to *collect, preserve, exhibit,* and *educate*—and has achieved national and international recognition along the way. The collection has doubled in the past four decades and now includes some 89,000 objects. The museum's nearly two hundred rooms have allowed us to keep most of this collection on permanent exhibit. The institution's conservation offices and laboratories, which opened in 1969, have spurred research and treatments that have contributed significantly to the preservation field. And Winterthur has worked steadily to expand its educational role, serving a diversified audience. In addition to a variety of tours for the drop-in visitor, Winterthur offers special-subject and special-needs tours, multilevel school tours, three graduate degree programs (cosponsored with the University of Delaware), annual, biennial, and occasional conferences and symposia, and numerous publications.

Winterthur is perhaps best known for its period room installations. When the museum opened, its first curator, Joseph Downs, recognized that period rooms gave the museum "a unique intimacy." That intimacy, which Winterthur has maintained in the face of increasing public demand to see the collection, is founded on a unique exhibition philosophy: individual objects are displayed in sympathetic domestic settings, enabling visitors to see, study, and appreciate them in historical and aesthetic contexts.

In the 1980s the Winterthur staff and trustees decided that by creating gallery exhibition spaces the institution could complement the existing period-room settings, better serve the current audience, and introduce American decorative arts to new audiences. Gallery spaces would also allow Winterthur to offer visitors stimulating ways of thinking about the decorative arts and their connection with the past.

The challenge of designing the first exhibition for Winterthur's new gallery was daunting. The staff and board of trustees wanted it to be representative of the museum's vast collection, current scholarship, and commitment to quality. Curators Philip D. Zimmerman and Donald L. Fennimore were successive chairmen of the task force that was assigned this challenge. They and their colleagues conceived, designed, and installed a comprehensive exhibition that embodies an enormously creative approach to the breadth and depth of the museum's collection.

Philip Zimmerman also wrote the catalogue, which highlights more than 150 objects that illustrate the exhibition's six major themes:

Change over Place, Change over Time, Technique and Technology, Maker and Marketplace, Ritual and Custom, and Messages and Symbols. As his text explains, these themes provide opportunities to view and review objects in ways that are rich in history, culture, appreciation and understanding, and enjoyment. On a more subtle level, his essay supports a multiperspective approach to the decorative arts that replaces the long-standing assumption that museums best serve their visitors by displaying collections according to style periods or some other single point of view. Although inherently more complex, the multiperspective approach unlocks the diversity and abundance of meaning that objects have and appeals to the similarly varied interests and experiences of the audience. Philip Zimmerman's lavishly illustrated essay is designed to be read on a variety of levels, ranging from a focus on the illustrations to a scrutiny of the sources informing his argument.

We hope all who view the exhibition in person and those who sample it from an armchair will find the new facets of Winterthur challenging, rewarding, and exciting.

Thomas A. Graves, Jr.
Director
March 1992

Fig. 1. A desk-and-bookcase may be understood and appreciated from many different perspectives. This desk of Boston manufacture, 1740–55, is made of mahogany with sabico, white pine and red cedar secondary woods and is 96 ⅜ inches high (acc. 60.1134). Inscribed in ink on the bottom of the top drawer behind the prospect door is "This desk was / purchased by / Josiah Quincy / o Braintree / 1778." Among other inscriptions is "John Allen his desk / Made [illegible]" scratched into top of desk section and "[illegible] / his desk August 1791" in ink on back of prospect drawer case.

Introduction

Why bother with things? What do people see in these objects that gives them value and meaning? We surround ourselves with objects and use them every day. They shape our physical world and establish our place in our communities and culture. When these objects no longer satisfy our needs, we alter them or make new ones. We change their shapes and decoration or use them differently: a more "stylish" table replaces an old-fashioned one; a dinner plate becomes a coaster for a potted plant. These changing configurations of objects, therefore, become records of human existence and significant sources for historical and cultural interpretation.[1]

People have taken many different approaches in their efforts to discover the meanings of decorative arts objects. This essay and the exhibition it accompanies seek to affirm a pluralistic view of the decorative arts in early America by recognizing six particular points of view or ways of understanding these objects that represent current trends in scholarship.[2]

A first step in studying decorative arts objects is to determine what they are. To learn their various characteristics and gain insight about them, we may examine objects and note certain physical properties—material, construction techniques, and condition. Careful visual inspection is usually sufficient, but some questions are resolved better by use of scientific procedures such as x-radiography, microscopic examination of samples, or spectroanalysis.

The functions that objects serve and their individual histories are intangible attributes rather than physical ones. Properly recognized and described, they may suggest meaningful links to broader questions or concerns about the culture that produced them and, by reflection, our culture. Most objects have multiple functions, some of which may change over time. For example, an antique desk-and-bookcase once owned by Josiah Quincy may continue to function as an object of beauty and status, but if it becomes part of a museum collection, its function as a writing surface and place to store personal papers will likely cease (fig. 1).

An object's history influences its significance, value, and meaning. Careful determination of the record of change in an object, including changes in ownership patterns and use, associa-tion with historic people or events, and changes in physical condition, introduces many potentially rewarding avenues for further investigation. For years the Quincy desk-and-bookcase was misunderstood as a product of the late 1770s because of a 1778 ownership inscription. More careful examination revealed the inscription to be one of several that detail historical circumstances, raising the possibility that others may have owned the piece before Quincy. Comparison and contrast of the desk-and-bookcase with related objects suggests a significantly earlier date of manufacture.[3] Its aesthetic qualities and technical features, including use of exotic woods, more accurately illuminate mid eighteenth-century, not revolutionary, Boston culture and craft.

Fortified with knowledge that identifies and describes what the objects are, we can investigate "how" and "why." Some subjects these questions address include: how people made or used particular objects, why certain objects were fashionable (and how that may compare to our aesthetic responses), and why tastes differed from place to place. By interpreting patterns of use, we can use objects to explore facets of everyday life and culture that are not well recorded in letters, diaries, public records, and other kinds of written evidence.

As with any research endeavor, the selection of objects influences our observations and conclusions. Because objects do not survive randomly, they may represent the past unevenly. Some objects survive because they have an association with an important person (from George Washington to a dear family member) or an event, while others may have been merely put aside and left undisturbed until they were rediscovered. Seldom, however, have our ancestors consciously collected and preserved objects to create an unbiased sample. The Winterthur collection is a case in point. Although seemingly encyclopedic in range and depth, it contains notable examples of decorative arts owned primarily by wealthy inhabitants of the Northeast and does not broadly represent the population. Within these limitations, it is an exceptionally rich source of knowledge and inspiration about our past, which is the foundation of our present.

---

[1] These concepts are addressed in Unit 1, "Why Things Matter," *The Material Culture of American Homes,* slide-tape series, Winterthur, 1985.

[2] As comprehensive as these six perspectives may seem, the decorative arts are open to even more avenues of inquiry and appreciation.

[3] See Brock Jobe, "A Boston Desk-and-Bookcase at the Milwaukee Art Museum," *Antiques* 140, no. 3 (September 1991): 413–19.

Change over Place

For decades, decorative arts historians have recognized that objects differ from place to place. Their efforts to document and plot these differences, such as those visible in the form and decoration of three eighteenth-century silver tankards made in Boston, New York, and Philadelphia (figs. 2, 3, 4), and to identify shared characteristics among objects can yield a rich map of regional patterns. In recent years, scholars from disciplines such as archaeology and cultural geography have investigated the relationships between people and place by asking how artifacts—objects, buildings, or even cityscapes—relate to a place and how specific geographical factors or conditions affected the design and fabrication of the artifacts made or used there. Analysis of this information reveals attitudes of taste, transmission of ideas, trade routes, ethnic identity, and a host of other factors that contribute to creating a cultural profile of a specific place.

Common designs, construction practices, and uses of particular materials define large regions in early America. For example, splat designs, carving, ways of modeling claw-and-ball feet, and other features distinguish regional expressions of Chippendale-style side chairs made in influential eighteenth-century regional centers (figs. 5, 6, 7, 8). Construction differences among these four chairs, such as types of joints and thickness of wood, also help to identify regional origin.

Figs. 2, 3, 4. Eighteenth-century silver tankards show regional differences in design. Fig. 2. Boston tankard by William Homes, Sr. or Jr., with a midrib encircling its tall body, 1760–80, H. 8½″ (acc. 80.111; gift of Mrs. C. Newbold Taylor). Fig. 3. New York tankard by Simeon Soumaine (ca. 1685–1750) with squat proportions, wide-brimmed crenelated lip, and cocoon-shaped thumbpiece, 1730–50, H. 6¾″ (acc. 63.524). Fig. 4. Philadelphia tankard by Philip Syng, Jr. (1703–89) having a pear-shaped body, 1745–89, H. 8¹⁄₁₆″ (acc. 61.620).

Figs. 5, 6, 7, 8. Chippendale-style side chairs with splat designs and carving common to their respective regions. Fig. 5. Boston, 1765–80, mahogany, H. 38″ (acc. 61.140.1). Fig. 6. Newport, R.I., 1760–85, mahogany, H. 38″ (acc. 59.83.1). Fig. 7. New York City, 1755–85, mahogany with secondary woods of white pine and red oak, H. 38 ⅜″ (acc. 59.2828). Fig. 8. Philadelphia, 1770–80, mahogany, H. 39″ (acc. 61.809.1).

Fig 2

Fig 3

Fig 4

Fig 5

Fig 6

Fig 7

Fig 8

Fig 9

Fig 10

Similarly, secondary woods—woods used in places that are not readily visible, such as interior blocks strengthening corners of a frame—demonstrate consistent selection of local materials.[4] The glazes used on stonewares reflecting availability of materials as well as localized practices also can be regionally distinctive (fig. 9).

Within a predominantly Anglo-American culture, some regional identities and expressions reflect the persistence of ties to continental European communities and places, particularly in French-, Dutch-, German-, and Swedish-speaking regions. Germanic influences, for example, are visible in the form, the shapes of the arms and front legs, and the carved decoration of a mid eighteenth-century upholstered armchair made in Lancaster, Pennsylvania (fig. 10), while an extraordinary early nineteenth-century tall clock, incorporating English and German words and many pictorial inlays of both patriotic and folk character, illustrates the forces of separation, accommodation, and assimilation between two cultural worlds that coexisted in Pennsylvania (fig. 11).[5]

[4] Two examples of research into regionalism are Henry Glassie, *Pattern in the Material Folk Culture of the Eastern United States* (Philadelphia: University of Pennsylvania Press, 1968); and Philip D. Zimmerman, "Regionalism in American Furniture Studies," in *Perspectives on American Furniture,* ed. Gerald W. R. Ward (New York: W. W. Norton, 1988), pp. 11–38. For fuller discussion of regional differences in eighteenth-century chairs, see John Kirk, *American Chairs: Queen Anne and Chippendale Early American Furniture* (New York: Alfred A. Knopf, 1972). The use of secondary woods to regionalize American furniture is pioneered in Charles F. Montgomery, *American Furniture: The Federal Period* (New York: Viking Press, 1966), pp. 27–40.

[5] Delaware valley turned chairs (illustrated below [figs. 66, 67, 68] in Maker and Marketplace) show Germanic influences in their arched slats and double undercut arms. See Benno M. Forman, "German Influences in Pennsylvania Furniture," in Scott T. Swank et al., *Arts of the Pennsylvania Germans,* ed. Catherine E. Hutchins (New York: W. W. Norton, 1983), pp. 103–4, 119–23.

Fig. 9. Stoneware vessels show regional uses of materials such as the use of an ash glaze instead of a salt glaze. *Left:* Albany, N.Y., jar with salt glaze, Paul Cushman, 1809, H. 10¾″ (acc. 58.1100). *Middle:* Edgefield, SC., jar with ash glaze, ca. 1840, H. 12⁹⁄₁₆″ (acc. 75.105; puchased with funds from the Claniel Foundation). *Right:* Boston, jug with salt glaze and with cobalt blue decoration, probably Jonathan Fenton, 1793–96, H. 11⅝″ (acc. 55.61.8).

Fig. 10. Germanic upholstered armchair. Probably Lancaster, Pa., 1750–75, black walnut with red pine secondary wood, H. 47″ (acc. 58.65).

Fig. 11. German American tall clock. Case: John Paul, Jr. (1789–1868), Lykens Township (Elizabethville), Dauphin County, Pa., 1815, maple, black walnut, inlays; works: brass; H. 98″. Works: brass. (acc. 58.2874).

Fig. 11

Regional centers influenced the material life in surrounding towns, in hamlets, and on farms. These centers, which were usually markets for the area or occasionally for particular products, were typically, but not always, thriving cities. They supported a significantly wider range of economic and cultural activities than their hinterlands and, for people living in those outlying places, served as a source of ideas, materials, and skills. Thus, urban objects, represented by a dressing table made in Salem, Massachusetts (fig. 12), established basic forms and decorative principles that could inspire reinterpretations, evident in an example from western Massachusetts (fig. 13). Urban influences on rural designs also are apparent in two pictures of General Washington (figs. 14, 15). The differences are greater than those attributable to the technical skills of each artist; the presentation of the subject—rendered in lifelike, three-dimensional qualities in the one and flattened in the other—points to differences in what was aesthetically acceptable to the purchasers. Itinerant New England portrait painter William Prior recognized this and in 1831 advertised: "Persons wishing for a flat picture can have a likeness without shade or shadow at one quarter price" of what he would charge for more realistic rendering.[6]

[6] Quoted in Nina Fletcher Little, "William M. Prior, Traveling Artist," *Antiques* 53, no. 1 (January 1948): 45. Thanks to E. McSherry Fowble and Barbara C. Shellenberger for their help in locating this quotation.

Figs. 12, 13. Urban and rural Massachusetts dressing tables. Fig. 12. Probably Salem, Mass., 1740–70, maple and birch with secondary woods of white pine and chestnut, H. 31 ¾" (acc. 59.839). Fig. 13. Northampton, Mass., area, 1765–80, cherry with secondary woods of white pine and yellow pine, H. 32" (acc. 58.589).

Fig 12

Fig 13

Fig. 14. *General George Washington Reviewing the Western Army at Fort Cumberland . . . ,*
by Frederick Kemmelmeyer (w. 1788–1816), Annapolis, Md., 1794, oil on paper, H. 18 ⅛″ (acc. 58.2780).

Fig. 15. *Washington at Verplanck's Point,* by John Trumbull (1756–1843),
New York, 1790, oil on canvas, H. 30″ (acc. 64.2201).

Similar aesthetic choices appear in the subtler variations of silver cans (baluster-shaped mugs) from urban Boston and rural Long Island (figs. 16, 17).

In looking for the paths that new ideas take, and conversely the barriers that may hinder their transmission or may contain certain ideas within specific areas, researchers have explored export and import trade, use of design and pattern books, and migration of skilled workers. The historical causes of regionalism in America lie in relationships between the colonies and Europe, especially England. England provided language, religion, technology and learning, government, and other cultural dimensions, and it served as merchandiser of most objects used in the colonies. Substantial quantities of English ceramics, textiles, pewter, brass, silver, and other metal objects were exported to America (figs. 18, 19). Each object carried information about style and technology. Few objects reveal this relationship better than a stylish English-made pitcher of 1815–30 that Joseph Hemphill, owner of Philadelphia-based Tucker Porcelain Company, copied and produced in his name in 1833 (fig. 20).

Figs. 16, 17. Silver cans also had regionally different body shapes. Fig. 16. John Coburn (1724–1803), Boston, 1760–70. H. 5¼″ (acc. 72.1). Fig. 17. Elias Pelletreau (1726–1810), Southampton, N.Y., 1750–80. H. 5⅝″ (acc. 66.115).

Figs. 18, 19. English-made tobacco boxes imported for American use. Fig. 18. Probably England, ca. 1724, brass, H. 1⁹⁄₁₆″; owned by John Moore, Jr. (1686–1749), of New York City (acc. 57.98). Fig. 19. Sheffield, England, 1792–1800, brass and tin, H.¾″, owned by Solomon Gorgas, a clockmaker in Ephrata, Pa. (acc. 60.1207).

Fig. 20. American-made pitcher with an English prototype. "Joˢ. Hemphill / Philaⁱᵃ. / 1833" in overglaze red on bottom, Joseph Hemphill (1770–1842), Philadelphia, 1833, hard-paste porcelain, H. 8⁷⁄₁₆″ (acc. 74.33); probably Spode factory, Stoke-on-Trent, Staffordshire, England, 1815–1830, soft-paste porcelain, H. 7¼″ (acc. 72.114; gift of Joseph Y. Jeanes, Jr.).

Fig 16

Fig 17

16

Fig. 18

Fig. 19

Fig. 20

A design for a "horse fier [fire or pole] screen" in Thomas Sheraton's *Drawing Book*, published serially in London from 1791 to 1794, soon after inspired a furniture maker in Salem, Massachusetts (figs. 21, 22).

Yet a third route for the transmission of ideas was the influx of immigrant craftsmen from all over Europe. They brought with them countless ideas about how things should look and be made. In New York City, for example, the early nineteenth-century work of French-trained Charles-Honoré Lannuier was so distinctive that John Hewitt, another furniture maker, referred to "Lanuas Collum [Lannuier's column]" when describing furniture legs in his account book (fig. 23).

Figs. 21, 22. Fire screen with a drawing book prototype. Fig. 21. Salem, Mass., 1800–1815, mahogany and maple, H. 46½″ (acc. 57.656). Fig. 22. Thomas Sheraton, *The Cabinet-Maker and Upholsterer's Drawing-Book* (London 1793), appendix pl. 13.

Fig. 23. Pier table stamped by Lannuier and having brass-mounted tapered reeded legs showing his French-inspired version of a columnar leg. Charles-Honoré Lannuier (1779–1819), New York City, 1803–10, mahogany, brass, marble with secondary woods of white pine and tulip poplar, H. 36½″ (acc. 61.1693).

Fig. 21

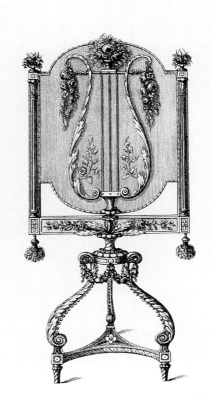

Fig. 22

18

Fig 23

Fig 24

Fig 25

Fig 26

Simon Chaudron, a Frenchman working in partnership with Anthony Rasch of Philadelphia, influenced early nineteenth-century American silver designs (fig. 24). Dutch immigrants and their descendants were well known for their excellent silvermaking and engraving in the late seventeenth and early eighteenth centuries (fig. 25). German-born John Frederick Amelung hired highly skilled glassmakers to work at his New Bremen Glass Manufactory near Frederick, Maryland, which produced the best American-made glass in the German *waldglass* tradition (fig. 26). An animalistic finial in the shape of a swan and crimped decoration on the handles of a fine Amelung covered sugar bowl distinguish it from bowls that follow English lead-glass-making traditions that relied on form and cut or faceted surfaces for decorative effect.

Fig. 24. French-inspired silver tea and coffee set. Simon Chaudron (ca. 1758–1846) and Anthony Rasch (ca. 1778–1857), Philadelphia, 1809–12 (acc. 75.80.1–.5; gift of Mr. and Mrs. Henry Pleasants in memory of Maria Wilkins Smith).

Fig. 25. New York silver bowl with chased panels of naturalistic ornament and cast handles characteristic of Dutch-American silver. Jacob Ten Eyck (1705–93), Albany, N.Y., 1726–50, H. 4⅝″ (acc. 55.127; gift of Charles K. Davis).

Fig. 26. Germanic *waldglas* sugar bowl. John Frederick Amelung (1741–98), New Bremen Glass Manufactory, New Bremen, Md., 1785–95, nonlead glass, H. 8½″ (acc. 52.279).

Change over Time

Designs and purposes of all kinds of objects change over time, and the reasons that certain objects or features appear, change, and disappear are as complex as the human forces that originally created them (fig. 27). Among the many reasons for change is fashion. When David Spear of Boston wrote to his fiancée Marcy Higgins in 1787 that "Mr. Bright . . . is to make all of the Mehogany Furniture . . . the Chairs are different from any you ever saw, but they are very pretty, of the newest Taste" (for example, see fig. 33), he was responding to a desire to participate in a social group that in part identified itself by the appearance of the things that its members owned and used. The expressive power of fashionable objects sometimes overcame personal preferences: while in London, Benjamin Franklin, for example, sent his wife four silver salt spoons that were in the "newest, but ugliest, Fashion."[7]

To make some sense of change and diversity on the one hand and continuity on the other, we often sort objects into broadly defined groups with related features. By recognizing patterns within these groupings based on certain characteristics of form and decoration, and by codifying principles and rules, we distinguish styles. Objects with known dates of manufacture provide evidence for establishing style dates and date ranges (fig. 28). This can lead to the conclusion, for example, that Spear was referring to federal-style shapes and decoration when he said that his chairs were in the "newest Taste."

[7] Quoted in Robert Bartlett Haas, "The Forgotten Courtship of David and Marcy Spear, 1785–1787," *Old-Time New England 52*, no. 3 (Winter 1962): 70. Spear likely refers to cabinetmaker George Bright (1727–1805) of Boston. Benjamin Franklin to Deborah Franklin, February 19, 1758, *The Papers of Benjamin Franklin*, vol. 7, *October 1, 1758, through March 31, 1758*, ed. Leonard W. Labaree (New Haven: Yale University Press, 1963), p. 381. Thanks to Charles F. Hummel for this reference.

Fig. 27

Fig. 27. Wineglasses showing design changes from 1700 to 1850. *Left to right:* England, 1700–1725, lead glass, H. 5¾″ (acc. 61.1334); Bohemia or Germany, 1720–30, nonlead glass, H. 5⅝″ (acc. 65.2444); England, ca. 1770, lead glass, H. 5⁵⁄₁₆″ (acc. 61.96); England, 1770–90, lead glass, H. 6¾″ (acc. 68.167); United States, 1830–50, lead glass, H. 5³⁄₁₆″ (acc. 81.247.1; gift of the estate of James O'Hara Cazenove).

Fig. 28. Datable porcelain cup and dated ceramic "sack" (white wine) jug. Cup: China, ca. 1610–12, porcelain with underglaze blue decoration, H. 1½″, salvaged from the cargo of *Witte Leew* [White Lion], a Dutch East India ship that sunk in 1613, and matches fragments excavated at Jamestown, Va. (acc. 78.28; purchased with funds from Mrs. Alfred P. Harrison); jug: Lambeth, England, 1648, tin-glazed earthenware with cobalt blue decoration, H. 8⅜″ (acc. 60.760).

Fig 28

The generally used "style periods" in early American decorative arts are based on objects that largely were made for and used by more prosperous Americans of English heritage, people who dominated the marketplace and many other aspects of the evolving culture (figs. 29, 30, 31, 32, 33, 34, 35).[8] Accordingly, this classification system provides an intellectual framework for their interpretation, but it is not the only one. There is a wide assortment of objects made for non-Anglo-Americans in all centuries. Swedish botanist Peter Kalm, who toured the colonies in 1749, noted diversity within objects made and used by Anglo-Americans as well as the striking differences in the houses and furnishings of people of Dutch and German heritage.

[8] For discussion of basic style names and characteristics, see Helen Comstock, *American Furniture: Seventeenth, Eighteenth, and Nineteenth Century Styles* (New York: Viking Press, 1962); Oscar P. Fitzgerald, *Three Centuries of American Furniture* (Englewood Cliffs, N.J.: Prentice-Hall, 1982); and Graham Hood, *American Silver: A History of Style, 1650–1900* (New York: Praeger Publishers, 1971).

Fig. 29. Seventeenth-century-style armchair. Essex County, Mass., 1640–85, red and white oaks, H. 36½″ (acc. 54.73).

Fig. 30. William and Mary-style side chair. Boston, 1700–1720, beech, original leather upholstery, H. 43½″ (acc. 81.46).

Fig. 31. Queen Anne-style side chair. Possibly by John Leach (d. 1799), Boston, 1735–60, black walnut, H. 40¼″ (acc. 54.523).

Fig. 32. Chippendale-style side chair. Boston, 1765–90, mahogany with white pine secondary wood, H. 36⅝″ (acc. 59.2639).

Fig. 33. Federal-style side chair. Labeled on back rail by Jacob Forster (1764–1838), Charlestown, Mass., 1795, mahogany, inlays with maple secondary wood, H. 37″ (acc. 60.349).

Fig. 34. Empire-style side chair. Boston, 1810–20, mahogany with birch secondary wood, horsehair upholstery, H. 33⅛″ (acc. 82.99.1; purchased with funds from Charles K. Davis).

Fig 29

Fig 32

Fig 30

Fig 31

Fig 33

Fig 34

A Pennsylvania-made box with Germanic designs does not relate directly to conventional Anglo-American style periods (fig. 36) and requires that we understand and appreciate its particular historical contexts.

The issue of style is further complicated by continuity: the persistent use of certain designs, forms, materials, or other properties that express style in objects. Objects of different "style" periods have "style" features that overlap, and there is no consistent rate of change over time. For example, some side chairs made after 1770 had a fashionable "Chippendale"-style splat and crest rail but older-style "William and Mary" legs (fig. 37). The latter did not necessarily make the chair old-fashioned. Because these chairs omitted any features of the Queen Anne style (which came in between), we cannot identify them as "transitional," a term that implies that the objects are between consecutive styles. In recent years some scholars have used "vernacular" to describe objects whose various design properties exhibit persistence and continuity more clearly than sensitivity to "high style" standards of change. A cabinet illustrates how one craftsman employed a broad design vocabulary in ways that do not always conform to our twentieth-century sense of what "high style" was (fig. 38). This, too, may fall under the "vernacular" umbrella, but further refinement of an interpretive framework is necessary to understand these objects more fully from the perspective of time.

Fig. 35

Fig. 36

Fig. 35. Miniature sideboard with knifeboxes and silver tea set illustrating federal style forms and arrangement. (A coal scuttle sits on the floor in front.) Sideboard: Massachusetts, probably Boston area, 1800–1830, mahogany, mahogany veneer, inlays, and white pine as secondary wood, H. 13⅞" (acc. 59.995). English silver and knife boxes: shagreen (sharkskin), silver, various dates (acc. 55.136.38–39, .58, .60–61, .63–64, .70–71, .74, .77, 59.996–97, .1034–35). Overall height of sideboard and knifeboxes as illustrated: 19".

Fig. 36. Pennsylvania German box. Probably Bern Township, Pa., tulip poplar, H. 9¹⁄₁₆"; "1785" painted on front and "FE.BERY / 1785 / .CA. SL" painted on bottom (acc. 59.2806).

Fig. 37. Vernacular side chair showing persistence in design details. New Hampshire or northeastern Massachusetts, 1770–1800, maple, H. 37⅛"; stamped "J.F.BLY." (a later owner) on underside of rear stretcher (acc. 54.2.2).

Fig. 38. Small cabinet. Probably Connecticut, 1800–1820, maple and pine, H. 20¹⁄₁₆" (acc. 72.436; gift of Charles van Ravenswaay).

Fig 38

Fig 37

Fig 39

Understanding objects in relation to change over time allows us to relate them to changes in living patterns and in technology. Four examples illustrate this. New interests in drinking tea and in playing cards inspired new table forms in the 1730s and 1740s. Changing sleep and rest habits resulted in the disappearance of daybeds in the late eighteenth century. The Windsor chair, comprised of legs and a back inserted into a thick plank seat, represented a radical departure in chair design attributable to new technology (fig. 39).[9] In metalworking, the technological development that combined drawing and silver-plating wire into a single, inexpensive process led to more delicate designs, as a pair of silver-plated candlesticks whose structural support and aesthetic design depend on the wire strings of the lyre exemplify (fig. 40).

Although some objects express time-sensitive features clearly and may be dated exactly, others require keen investigation, sometimes involving seemingly unimportant factors, to understand them properly from the perspective of time. Some fashionable European-made objects introduced new design concepts and forms that, to the colonists, may have appeared incongruous in their American homes (fig. 41), which explains why merchants and craftsmen retailing these wares regularly touted them as "entirely new," "remarkable," "never-before-seen," and "curious." If we use benchmark American-made decorative arts as our only guide, the dates that we assign these English goods would likely be too late.

[9] The earliest reference to American Windsors appears in a 1748 Philadelphia newspaper advertisement. See Nancy Goyne Evans, "Design Sources for Windsor Furniture," pt. 1, "The Eighteenth Century," *Antiques* 133, no. 1 (January 1988): 283.

Fig. 39. Windsor armchair. Philadelphia, 1750–65, oak, ash, tulip poplar, and maple, H. 44¾″ (acc. 78.106).

Fig. 40. Pair of lyre-shaped candlesticks. England, probably Sheffield, 1780–1800, silver plate on copper, H. 13¼″ (acc. 59.1597–98).

Fig. 41. Snuff box with rococo engraving. "Robert Jaffray / 1743" engraved on top, Thomas Lakin, Birmingham, England, steel, H.¾″ (acc. 59.1890).

Fig. 40

Fig. 41

Fig 42

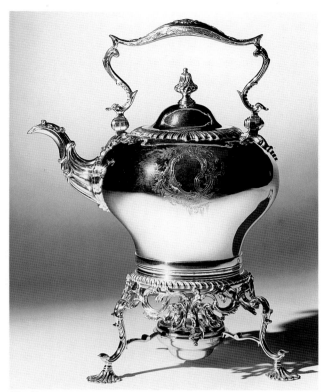

Fig 43

Fig 44

Fig 45

But the reverse is also true. Style characteristics can suggest dates that are much earlier than that object's actual time of manufacture. Winterthur's Queen Anne-style high chest made in Stratford, Connecticut, dates from 1784, not fifty years earlier (fig. 42), and the touchmarks on a Philadelphia rococo-style kettle indicate that it was made in the 1820s, not in the 1750s and 1760s (fig. 43). In each case, these objects were expensive and intended for prominent locations in the home. Their well-to-do buyers preferred styles that were fully a generation or more old, suggesting how persistent and popular certain designs might be.

Further complicating the issue of change over time are objects whose form and decoration carry little or no time-sensitive information (figs. 44, 45). These objects are often inexpensive or utilitarian wares with little ornamentation, or they are ornamented with certain motifs or with decorating techniques that remained unchanged for decades. Since conjectural dating of these objects is a problematic exercise that is unlikely to enhance our understanding or appreciation of them, we should interpret their aesthetic, cultural, or historical qualities from other perspectives.

Fig. 42. Queen Anne-style high chest dated 1784. "1784 made / August 1784 Brewster Dayton made theese draws / at Stratford" inscribed in chalk on inside back board of upper case. Brewster Dayton (d. 1797) Stratford, Conn., cherry with secondary woods of pine and tulip poplar, H. 86¾" (acc. 68.772).

Fig. 43. Rococo-style tea kettle made in the 1820s. Edward Lownes, Philadelphia, 1817–34, silver, H. 14⅞" (acc. 51.50).

Fig. 44. Colander, an object whose form, materials, and decoration did not change over time. Probably Pennsylvania, probably nineteenth century, glazed red earthenware, H. 5" (acc. 60.109).

Fig. 45. Stool, an object whose design makes no reference to a particular style. Probably southern United States, probably nineteenth century, bald cypress and ash, H. 22¾" (acc. 59.1815).

Techniques and Technology

In 1678 Joseph Moxon of London began printing *The Mechanick Exercises* in which he described basic tools and processes for many crafts. He found an eager audience, and his material remained in print through 1703. By observing that "one Trade may borrow many Eminent Helps in Work of another Trade," Moxon recognized that particular techniques are not defined only by specific crafts.[10] Three centuries later curiosity about the "art and mystery" of crafts remains strong, perhaps enhanced by the numbers of objects surviving from earlier times that are no longer made and used. An understanding of craft techniques, which in turn affects how an object appears, makes the decorative arts more accessible.

Various inlay techniques, for example, were used in different trades and with different materials (figs. 46, 47, 48, 49).

[10] Joseph Moxon, *The Mechanick Exercises; or, The Doctrine of Handy-Works* (3d ed., 1703; reprint, New York: Praeger Publishers, 1970), preface. Crafts include smithing, joinery, house carpentry, turning, bricklaying, and sundial making.

Figs. 46, 47. Tumbler decorated with sulphide bust of Benjamin Franklin inlaid in base. Bakewell, Page and Bakewell (1808–82), Pittsburgh, Pa., ca. 1825, lead glass, H. 3⅜″ (acc. 57.76.1).

Fig. 48. Detail of a butterfly inlay on the drawer front of a dressing glass. New Jersey, 1800–1820, mahogany, inlays, H. (inlay) 2⅛″ (acc. 51.23).

Fig. 49. Turner decorated with three inlaid hearts. Probably southeastern Pennsylvania, 1800–1840, wrought iron, copper inlay, L. 13″ (acc. 65.1617).

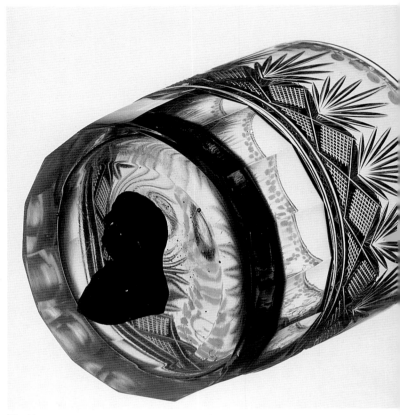

Fig. 46

Fig. 47

Fig 48

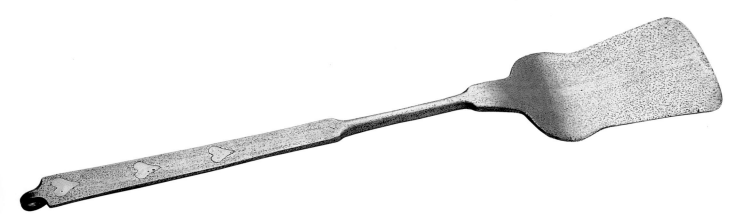

Fig 49

Fig 50

Fig 51

Relationships among different trades based on commonly used techniques are also apparent in turning, a process that involves removing material from objects rotating on a fixed axis. Turning is fundamental to much furniture making in the manufacture of structural and decorative elements (fig. 50). Turning was also used by brass- and coppermakers, who cast candlesticks and other cylindrical objects and then placed them on lathes to skim the surfaces with "hooks" that sharpened the contours (fig. 51). Potters have used another kind of turning, evident in the making of a mochaware "engine-turned" bowl in which the geometric, ringed decoration was applied by a regulated turning mechanism (fig. 52). Carving, cutting, and engraving—all techniques that rely on freehand removal of material from a surface—represent other processes common to crafts as diverse as pottery making, glassmaking, printing, wood-carving, and metalworking.

Fig. 50. Chest with one drawer, decorated with pairs of applied split turnings. Symonds shop tradition, Salem or Rowley, Mass., 1660–90, red oak, black walnut, maple, and white pine, H. 28¾" (acc. 58.688).

Fig. 51. Candlestick with skimming marks visible around the candle socket and the underside of the base. Germany or the Netherlands, seventeenth century, brass, H. (standing upright) 9¼" (acc. 54.554).

Fig. 52. Engine-turned bowl whose decoration was cut into the sides of the body by a rotating device that regulates a cutting point in a variety of patterns. Staffordshire, England, 1800–1825, pearlware, H. 3½" (acc. 70.180).

Fig. 52

Basic techniques for shaping clay into finished ceramic forms include "throwing," or raising, on a potter's wheel and casting slip (a watered clay) into molds (figs. 53, 54). Casting, a process of giving shape to liquified materials by pouring them into a mold and letting them harden without pressure, and raising are also essential techniques in metalworking. Silversmiths cast parts and whole objects, ranging from small finials to large platters (fig. 55). They also "raise" hollowware forms by repeatedly hammering silver disks and slowly turning them by hand (figs. 56, 57).[11]

[11] A parallel form of turning occurs with spinning, a process employed by pewterers to make vessels from sheets of britannia – an alloy of tin, antimony, and copper – by turning the disks on a lathe and shaping them against wooden forms. Although this technology was available by the early 1800s, the relatively few surviving examples of spun pewter suggest that most pewterers continued to cast and skim the metal.

Fig. 53. Thrown ceramic bowl. New England, probably eastern Massachusetts, eighteenth century, glazed earthenware, H. 3½″ (acc. 60.312).

Fig. 54. Porous molds used in slip casting were made (and remade) from master molds. Finely rendered surface details of this master mold for a cup contrast with the less distinct surface qualities on a similar cup. (The casting process and application of glaze both contributed to the softer design details on the cup.) Mold: Staffordshire, England, 1740–60, stoneware, H. 3⅝″ (acc. 70.424; gift of Mr. and Mrs. John Mayer). Cup: possibly Aaron Wood (1718–85), Burslem, Staffordshire, England, 1740–60, salt-glazed stoneware, H. 2¹¹⁄₁₆″ (acc. 58.873).

Fig. 55. Faint hallmarks below the rim indicate that the form of this slip-cast porcelain creamer was taken directly from an English silver creamer of 1773/74 similar to the one shown. Porcelain creamer: probably Pennington Factory, Liverpool, England, ca. 1774, soft-paste porcelain, H. 4⅝″ (acc. 69.135). Silver creamer: Thomas Smith, London, England, 1752/53, silver, H. 4¾″ (acc. 80.195; gift of Marshall P. Blankarn).

Figs. 56, 57. Lettering visible along the rim indicates that the silversmith made this ladle from a silver coin, an Austrian thaler. Joseph Warner (1742–1800), Wilmington, Del., 1763–1800, silver, horn, L. 13⅝″ (acc. 82.89).

Fig. 53

Fig. 54

Fig 55

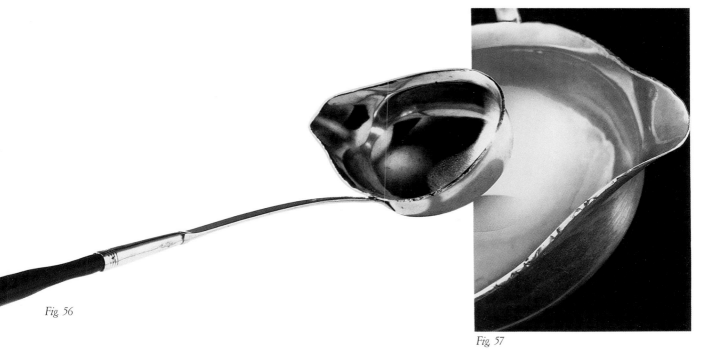

Fig 56

Fig 57

Despite the similarities in processes among the various trades, tools and specific skills necessary to execute them varied significantly and required substantial investments of money to acquire them and time to learn their use. Certain processes have few parallels in other trades. Glassblowing, for example, has been a singular skill among the many tasks required to produce glasswares (fig. 58). The great demand for glassblowers and their migratory life-styles contributed to their distinct identity among tradesmen. Some emphasized glassblowers' individuality further by characterizing them as being "addicted to carousing and extravagance."[12]

[12] Quoted in Arlene Palmer Schwind, "The Glassmakers of Early America," in *The Craftsman in Early America*, ed. Ian M. G. Quimby (New York: W. W. Norton, 1984), p. 180.

Fig. 58. Glassmakers' products were made by more than one process. *Left:* vase blown into a part-sized paneled mold; probably Boston and Sandwich Glass Company (1825–88) Sandwich, Mass., 1835–55, lead glass, H. 7 11/16″ (acc. 59.3140). *Middle:* free-blown bottle, probably midwestern United States, 1815–50, nonlead glass, H. 10¾″ (acc. 68.194; gift of Charles van Ravenswaay). *Right:* blown and engraved pitcher having a tooled spout and applied handle. "W / I*E / 1810" engraved on body under spout, England or Ireland, 1810, lead glass, H. 6⅝″ (acc. 61.18).

Fig. 58

Changes in techniques and processes have an impact on the shape and use of objects and on everyday life and culture. Lighting is a good illustration.[13] In the seventeenth and early eighteenth centuries, common lighting devices were betty lamps, candlesticks, and taper sticks, all of which burned oils and animal fats (fig. 59). Adjustable, portable stands allowed individuals to set the light source close to the work at hand (fig. 60). From the 1780s through the 1860s, many technical improvements in wicks and in fuel refining led to higher and more even levels of illumination, reduced the risk of accidental fires, and lowered levels of smoke and sparks (figs. 61, 62). These changes affected routines of daily life by extending people's ability to read and carry out other activities in nondaylight hours and by providing more flexibility concerning where such activities could take place in the home.

[13] Some other areas of study include heating, transportation, and numerous developments in various crafts.

Fig. 59. The inner bowl of a crusie lamp (distinguished from a betty lamp by an outer bowl to catch drippings) held oil that burned at a wick placed in the spout. Probably England, eighteenth century, iron, H. as shown 7¾″ (acc. 59.1993).

Fig. 60. The ratchet design of some stands allowed a user to adjust the height of the burning candle for best illumination. Stand: possibly New England, 1750–1800, maple and white pine, H. (as illustrated) 25¾″ (acc. 60.741). Candlestick: probably Birmingham, England, 1750–70, brass, H. 8¼″ (acc. 58.1902).

Fig. 61. The cylindrical burners of argand lamps produced bright and steady light; the refined oils, gravity fed from a reservoir to a burner that needed little adjustment, produced little soot or other residue. John Phipson and Abraham Lambley (1828–39), Birmingham, England, brass, iron, and glass, H. 20½″ (acc. 73.40.1–.2; purchased with funds from the Atwater Kent Foundation).

Fig. 62. The ring-shaped reservoir supporting the glass globe of a sinumbra lamp minimized shadows. Thomas Messenger and Sons (1829–46), Birmingham, England, 1829–46, brass, iron, and glass, H. 27¾″ (acc. 75.223; purchased with funds from the Claniel Foundation).

Fig 60

Fig 59

Fig. 61

Fig 62

Maker and Marketplace

Account books, price books, trade catalogues, and estate inventories present data on monetary values that makers and users placed on objects. When we look at objects from this perspective, we focus on the role they played as commodities in a complex arena of exchange.[14] Makers needed to obtain raw materials, sometimes from distant sources. To fabricate these materials into finished goods, they drew on valuable training and skills, including those of other craftsmen, and used tools and equipment, some of which could be costly. Finally, purchasers had to buy. Newspaper advertisements and the existence of a few retail shops suggest that some individuals were actively creating markets, both locally and in distant communities, to enhance demand for their wares. Although much of what was produced in the colonial period was "bespoke" work (that is, made to satisfy a specific order), wares "ready made after the newest fashion" became increasingly available in urban areas after the mid eighteenth century. All of these participants combined to form a marketplace that, although different from today's, has many striking similarities and offers significant insight into early decorative arts and the forces that shaped them.

Objects result from many marketplace decisions and conditions such as choice, cost, availability, and marketing strategies (including advertising). To supply what a consumer was willing (or able) to pay, makers provided alternatives at various prices (figs. 63, 64).

[14] Recent studies on consumerism have increased our understanding of the role of objects in describing and defining culture. See, for example, Grant McCracken, *Culture and Consumption: New Approaches to the Symbolic Character of Consumer Goods and Activities* (Bloomington: Indiana University Press, 1988).

Figs. 63, 64. Inexpensive goods, such as this earthenware salt, were fashioned to imitate the form and decoration of more expensive objects, represented by this cut-glass salt. Fig. 63. Earthenware salt, England or United States, 1790–1820, glazed yellow earthenware, H. 3⅛″ (acc. 60.615). Fig. 64. Cut-glass salt: England or Ireland, 1790–1810, lead glass, H. 3⅝″ (acc. 69.1366).

Fig. 65. *(Overleaf pages 44, 45).* Seven plates suggesting the range of dinnerwares available in the 1810s. *Center:* Herculaneum Factory, England, 1800–1825, transfer-printed creamware, diam. 9⅝″ (acc. 59.588); *Clockwise from bottom left:* William Davenport & Co., Longport, England, 1793–1810, pearlware, diam. 9⅞″ (acc. 69.337.8; gift of Mrs. Alfred C. Harrison); China, 1800–1820, hard-paste porcelain with enamel decoration in "Fitzhugh" pattern, diam. 9¾″ (acc. 56.548.10); William Yale, Jr., and Samuel Yale (1813–20), Meriden, Conn., 1813–20, pewter, diam. 8⅜″ (acc. 56.59.8; gift of Joseph France); Staffordshire, England, 1800–1825, transfer-printed pearlware, diam. 8¼″ (acc. 78.81.1); probably France, 1810–20, porcelain with enamel and gilt decoration, diam. 8¼″ (acc. 73.164.10; gift of Mr. and Mrs. John Mayer); probably New England, eighteenth century, maple, diam. 9⁹⁄₁₆″ (acc. 58.125.3).

Fig 63

Fig 64

Fig 65

For utilitarian needs such as dinner and kitchen wares, as well as expensive furniture, silver, and fine textiles, consumers could select from a broad range of materials and levels of ornamentation (figs. 65, 66, 67, 68, 69).

Preindustrial makers employed production systems that relied in varying degrees on parts standardization, specialized labor, and other trade practices not generally associated with early American crafts. By interchanging standardized parts and patterns within their shops, makers could inexpensively multiply the variety of their products. This is readily apparent in numerous brass and pewter objects made up of separate cast elements. It is also apparent in specialist-supplied cast-silver decoration, wooden inlays and carved elements, and furniture parts. The interchangeable leg patterns on two different Chippendale-style chairs made in the same Massachusetts shop allowed their maker to supply what eighteenth-century price books described as side chairs with "cut through bannesters" and marlboro (straight) legs or "crooked" (cabriole) legs. The cost of carving or other "extraordinary work" on such chairs was added "in proporsion" (fig. 70).[15]

Fig. 66

[15] For metals, see Charles V. Swain, "Interchangeable Parts in Early American Pewter," *Antiques* 83, no. 2 (February 1963): 212–13. Lumber merchant Samuel Williams advertised in the *Pennsylvania Gazette* "mahogany and walnut tea table columns" September 9, 1767, and "two hundred sets of low and high post bedstead stuff, fit for immediate use" June 12, 1769, and "300 sets" of the same June 2, 1773. Philadelphia furniture maker David Evans recorded in his daybook that he bought "12 Setts of Bedstead Stuff" May 9, 1777. The earliest American price book, "A Table for Prices for Joiners' Work in Providence, R.I., in 1757," appears in Irving W. Lyon, *The Colonial Furniture of New England* (3d ed., 1925; reprint, New York: E. P. Dutton, 1977), pp. 265–66. A more complete example of a Philadelphia cabinetmaker's price book of 1772 is discussed in Martin Eli Weil, "A Cabinetmaker's Price Book," in *American Furniture and Its Makers: Winterthur Portfolio 13*, ed. Ian M. G. Quimby (Chicago: University of Chicago Press, 1979), pp. 176–92.

Fig. 67

Fig. 68

Fig. 69

Figs. 66, 67, 68, 69. The form and amount of decoration on four Delaware valley armchairs reflect different price ranges. Additional labor and materials made more ornate or complicated objects more costly. Fig. 66. Four-slat armchair, eastern Pennsylvania, 1725–75, maple, rush seat, H. 43″ (acc. 67.761). Fig. 67. Five-slat armchair: eastern Pennsylvania, 1725–75, maple rush seat, H. 45½″ (acc. 59.2382). Fig. 68. Six-slat armchair with cabriole legs, probably Solomon Fussell/William Savery shop tradition, Philadelphia, 1735–60, maple, rush seat, H. 45⅛″ (acc. 52.236). Fig. 69. Solid-splat armchair with cabriole legs, probably Solomon Fussell/William Savery shop tradition, Philadelphia, 1750–65, maple, rush seat, H. 44½″ (acc. 64.1523).

Fig. 70. A marlboro leg and a cabriole leg from two side chairs that are otherwise identical. Boston, 1765–90, of mahogany with maple as secondary wood. Cabriole-leg chair: H. 38″ (acc. 61.140.1; figure 5 shows a full view of another chair from this set). Marlboro-leg chair: H. 38¾″ (acc. 53.166.3).

Fig. 70

Fig 71

Craftsmen of different trades collaborated to make the complex and ornate goods that some wealthy buyers demanded. Furniture makers supplied clockmakers with cases; framemakers worked with glassmakers to produce looking glasses; textile manufacturers provided sumptuous fabrics to upholsterers; and brass founders made drawer pulls, hinges, and other furniture fittings. Specialists such as woodcarvers not only carved furniture but also produced the patterns used by iron founders to impress sand molds before casting (fig. 71). Large-scale ceramics firms employed engravers to prepare copperplates used to produce transfer-printed images for their mugs and plates (fig. 72).

Makers' marks and inscriptions help us unravel complex working relationships and illuminate some early marketing practices. Although the workplace was largely unregulated in America, marking styles and practices drew heavily from European conventions dictated by guilds and regulatory groups. In Europe these marks identified makers, places of business, and occasionally times of manufacture and quality of materials.

Fig. 71. Woodcarvers provided iron founders with wooden patterns that were used for making impressions in sand molds. Andiron: United States, 1840–70, iron, H. 17" (acc. 64.1546.1). Andiron pattern: United States, 1870–1900, wood, H. 20½" (acc. 88.27; gift of Edward B. Thomas).

Fig. 72. Robert Hancock was among a number of English engravers who made copperplates for transfer printing designs onto ceramics and porcelains. His transfer-printed signature, "RH. Worcester," is visible below the military emblem. A portrait of the King of Prussia appears on the other side. Worcester Porcelain Factory (1751–), Worcester, England, ca. 1757, soft-paste porcelain, H. 4¹¹⁄₁₆" (acc. 58.722).

Fig. 72

In the colonies, marks tended to identify the names of makers and occasionally places (figs. 73, 74). Marks also provided a convenient way to advertise. A fine pewter coffeepot by William Will, a Philadelphia pewterer of excellent reputation, carries marks with his name and city, thus informing anyone who might see the object where another like it could be acquired (figs. 75, 76). That Will marked this object also may have altered, if only modestly, how people perceived it: his object was not just a coffeepot, it was the product of a highly skilled craftsman.

Advertising—whether in newspapers, on bill heads (illustrating different wares that presumably were available through that source), on printed labels, or on signs—invested objects with additional meanings by associating them with names, places, ideas, or other cultural values. Makers hoped that fashionability might stimulate demand. Manipulation of these associations might also enhance an object's market value in the minds of potential consumers. The Will coffeepot, for example, although made in Philadelphia, is also stamped "LONDON," apparently to suggest to potential buyers that Will's work was equal in quality to London wares, which enjoyed a worldwide reputation.

Figs. 73, 74. "SEMPER EADEM" appears with "LONDON" on the bottom of one pewter plate, and with "BOSTON" on a second plate. Spectro-analysis revealed that the "London"-stamped plate was of a low-quality pewter alloy similar to products made in Bristol, England (some of which were also stamped "London"). Researchers must now determine whether the "Semper Eadem" pewterer was a Bristol emigrant who carried his craft and goods with him or was a Boston craftsman who imported low-quality, unmarked wares that he then stamped "London" to suggest a higher quality. Fig. 75. "London" plate, probably England, 1760–80, 64% tin and 29% lead, diam. 8½" (acc. 56.59.14; gift of Joseph France); "Boston" plate, Boston, 1760–80, 90% tin and 7% lead, diam. 7¹³⁄₁₆" (acc. 56.59.12; gift of Joseph France).

Figs. 75, 76. A "LONDON" mark, stamped into the inside bottom walls of this fine coffeepot at the time of its manufacture, appears in addition to the touchmark "WM WILL / PHILADELPHIA," suggesting that maker William Will (1742–98) took advantage of the known quality of London wares. Philadelphia, 1780–98, pewter, H. 15⅞" (acc. 54.33).

Fig 73

Fig 74

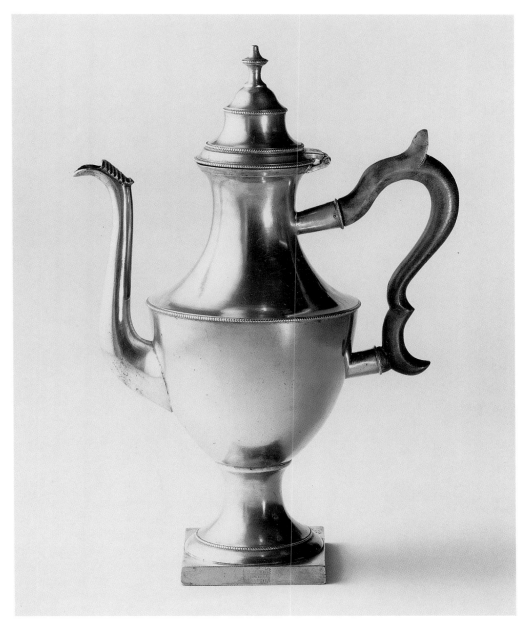

Fig 75

Fig 76

51

Fig. 77. This gentleman's secretary, dating from 1795–98 and labeled on the back of each case section by cabinetmaker Nehemiah Adams (1769–1840) of Salem, Mass., was found in Capetown, South Africa, where it was owned throughout the nineteenth century. Mahogany, mahogany veneer, inlays, and secondary woods of white pine and red cedar, H. 90″ (acc. 57.796).

Colonial craftsmen joined retailers and factors in market speculation. In the first half of the eighteenth century, furniture makers began advertising "ready-made" wares, sold their goods to neighboring towns and hinterlands, and occasionally shipped products to distant markets. In 1742, for example, Plunkett Fleeson of Philadelphia, responding to competitive imports, advertised that he had "Several Sorts of good Chair-frames, black and red leather Chairs, finished cheaper than any made here, or imported from Boston." Shipping records and account books of the 1750s and 1760s indicate that furniture makers from Newport, Rhode Island, to Portsmouth, New Hampshire, shipped large numbers of chairs and case furniture south as far as the Carolinas and West Indies and north as far as Newfoundland and Nova Scotia.[16]

By 1800 New England coastal furniture-making centers supported many craftsmen who engaged in "adventures," shipping their goods across the North and South Atlantic (fig. 77). In 1804 Nehemiah Adams shipped on the *Franklin* twenty-one pieces of furniture, including an expensive gentleman's secretary, two other secretaries, and nine lady's writing desks, and instructed the captain to sell them "for the most they will fetch at the Isle of France (Mauritius) [off the east coast of Africa] or elsewhere."[17] These same cabinetmakers also imported and sold foreign furniture, from Europe or made in the Orient to Western designs, in their market regions (fig. 78).

[16] Fleeson advertisement, *Pennsylvania Gazette*, September 23, 1742. Fleeson was an upholsterer who apparently employed chairmakers. For examples of furniture being exported to other regions see, Jeanne Vibert Sloane, "John Cahoone and the Newport Furniture Industry," and Brock W. Jobe, "An Introduction to Portsmouth Furniture of the Mid-Eighteenth Century," *Old-Time New England* 72, *New England Furniture* (1987), pp. 90–91 and 164–65; and Brock Jobe, "The Boston Furniture Industry, 1720–1740," in *Boston Furniture of the Eighteenth Century*, Publications of the Colonial Society of Massachusetts 48 (Boston, 1974), pp. 4–5. Sales and consignments of late eighteenth-century Philadelphia silver to silversmiths and agents in the Carolinas are described in Harrold C. Gillingham, "Philadelphia Silverware in the South," *Antiques* 31, no. 1 (January 1937): 22–23. Additional research will likely broaden our understanding of this kind of trade.

[17] William Appleton and Josiah Austin shared ownership in this vnture. Other Salem cabinetmakers actively engaged in export trade at this time included William Hook, Edmund Johnson, and Jacob and Elijah Sanderson (see "Furniture Exported by Cabinetmakers of Salem" from notes left by Henry Wyckoff Belknap published in *Essex Institute Historical Collections* 85 [1949]: 335–59).

Fig. 78. This Grecian-style couch is labeled on the frame by Thomas Needham of Salem, Massachusetts, but the design details, which differ from those on other furniture made in Salem during the early nineteenth century, and the use of caning to support loose cushions suggest that the couch was made in China for the Western market. Needham was among a number of Salem cabinetmakers active in trade with the Orient. Ca. 1820, mahogany with aspen secondary wood, H. 30¾" (acc. 57.575).

Many of the more expensive objects used in early America were imported by merchants. Peter Kalm observed in 1748: "England, and especially London, profits immensely by its trade with the American colonies; for not only in New York but likewise all the other English towns on the continent import so many articles from England that all their specie, together with the goods which they get in other countries must all go to Old England to pay their accounts there, for which they are, however, insufficient."[18] Some imports arrived as speculation, and others were special ordered. As the decades passed, foreign manufacturers began making objects with specific meaning for Americans, such as numerous images of George Washington and fellow patriots, historic events, and notable places on clocks, ceramics, and glasswares, to encourage sales in American markets. Many special orders augmented the voluminous trade with the Orient in particular. Factors, acting for American merchants, arranged to have porcelain wares brightly decorated with initials, armorial devices, or specialized motifs (fig. 79). When completed, these higher-priced special orders accompanied the tons of blue-and-white Canton and Nanking porcelains, teas, silks, and other wares bound for ready markets in America.

[18] November 2, 1748, entry in *Peter Kalm's Travels in North America*, vol. 1 (1770; reprint, New York: Dover Publications, 1966), p. 134.

Fig. 79. This fruit basket, decorated with "SOCIETAS CINCNNATORUM [sic] INSTITUTA.1783" and the initials "SS," was probably made for Samuel Shaw (1754–94), a revolutionary war officer and secretary to the Order of Cincinnati, who sailed to the Orient in 1784 as supercargo aboard the *Empress of China*. China, 1784–90, hard-paste porcelain, H. 14⅞" (acc. 59.2934).

Fig 79

Ritual and Custom

Objects contribute significantly to the practice of many daily routines, as well as the enactment of special occasions. When used to perform various social tasks or to give shape to the physical setting, they may acquire additional layers of meaning. In 1724 Samuel Sewell of Boston noted in his diary: "Deacon Checkly Deliver'd the Cup first to Madam Winthrop, and then gave me a Tankard. 'Twas humiliation to me and I think put me to the Blush to have this injustice done me by a Justice."[19] The source of Sewell's quiet outrage was not limited to the order in which he received communion. Standing cups signified a higher social level than did tankards, and the vessel he was offered violated his sense of his identity and importance (fig. 80). The study of objects from this perspective yields insight into attitudes, social identity, and changing customs and values.

Object design and availability influence social behavior, and specific requirements for use inspire new object forms and variations. Posset pots, card tables, and champagne glasses represent particular forms of objects whose identification is linked directly to tasks or functions. The long spouts of posset pots draw blended posset from the bottom of the bowl rather than curdled liquids at the top, and their two-handled design facilitates the passing of this communal drinking vessel from person to person (fig. 81).

[19] December 6, 1724, entry in Samuel Sewall, *Diary, 1674–1729*, ed. M. Halsey Thomas, vol. 2 (New York: Farrar, Straus, and Giroux, 1973), p. 1023.

Fig. 80. Standing cups were medieval drinking vessels whose form continued to be used in celebrations of Holy Communion. This example was probably made for a church in central Pennsylvania. Johann Christoph Heyne (1715–81), Lancaster, Pa., 1760–80, pewter, H. 10¹¹⁄₁₆″ (acc. 53.97; gift of Edgar Sittig).

Fig. 81. Posset pots were named for a hot drink of sweetened and spiced milk curdled with ale or wine. The coat of arms and motto "FIDELETER" (fidelity) faced the user and reminded him of the status of the pot's owner. Delftfield Pottery (1748–1823) or Glasgow Pottery (1764–84), Delftfield or Glasgow, Scotland, 1749–75, tin-glazed earthenware, H. 11½″ (acc. 57.536).

Fig. 80

Fig 81

Many use-specific objects are adaptations of existing forms: makers of card tables drew on hinged table-leaf and swing-leg techniques to create a table that would stand against a wall when not in use (fig. 82). Glassblowers elongated the wineglass form to enhance the effervescent qualities of champagne (fig. 83).

To assert social identity, people of means combined costly furniture, textiles, silver, and ceramics into displays of wealth and finery, and many of these arrangements of an individual's furnishings conformed to broadly accepted practices (fig. 84). At the end of the eighteenth century, Moreau de St. Méry commented while visiting Philadelphia: "Before dinner and all during dinner, as is the English custom, all the silver one owns is displayed on the sideboard in the dining room" (see fig. 35).[20]

[20] *Moreau de St. Méry's American Journey [1793–1798]*, trans. and ed. Kenneth Roberts and Anna M. Roberts (Garden City, N.Y.: Doubleday, 1947), p. 266.

Fig. 82. New York card tables typically were made with a fifth leg attached to a swinging rail that supported the hinged top. The playing surface of the top was often covered with baize or leather and had oval recesses for counters. 1770–90, mahogany with secondary woods of white pine and tulip poplar, H. 27½″ (acc. 58.1791).

Fig. 83. Champagne glass. United States, England, or Ireland, 1815–35, lead glass, H. 6⅞″ (acc. 68.128.10).

Fig. 84. The garniture displayed on a high chest top added beauty to the home as well as suggesting the sophisticated taste of its owner. Some early high chests had stepped tops to better display smaller ceramics, silver, and other appropriate belongings. Garniture: Holland, 1750–80, tin-glazed earthenware, H. of taller vases 13⅞″ (acc. 66.716.1–5). High chest: "J.M. / 1720" inscribed in chalk on backboard of upper case, probably Mass., ca. 1720, birch, maple and walnut veneers, with white pine as secondary wood (acc. 66.1306).

Fig 82

Fig 83

Fig 84

As rituals and customs changed, selection of appropriate objects for drinking and dining, leisure, personal care, and so forth also changed. The special uses and meanings associated with these objects provide clues that allow us to comprehend the patterns of social behavior in which they were used as well as the larger settings in which people lived. Studying objects from this perspective becomes more valuable in light of limited historical evidence concerning everyday life that is often richer in surviving objects than in written commentary.

From the late seventeenth to the early nineteenth centuries, the number of objects used for preparing and taking meals increased substantially. While this change reflects increased prosperity and improved technology and productivity, the many new kinds of tablewares also point to increased specialization and changes in eating habits caused by more widely shared views of proper etiquette (figs. 85, 86).[21] Their size and form distinguished dinner plates from dessert plates, wineglasses from water glasses, and many other objects—from small butter knives to large soup tureens—that helped to orchestrate the taking of meals.

[21] Changes in diet and increased availability of a greater variety of foods also may have influenced eating patterns.

Fig. 85. Late seventeenth-century place settings for two along with a charger (serving platter), pitcher, and standing salt. Various places and dates of manufacture, pewter, horn, wood, earthenware.

Fig. 86. Early nineteenth-century (ca. 1810–25) place settings for two with serving dishes, decanter, cruet stand, and candelabra. Various places and dates of manufacture, silver, glass, porcelain.

Fig. 85

Fig. 86

Fig 87

The settings that people created with objects also provide avenues to investigate how they managed daily life. Elaborate furniture forms and an assortment of objects related to dressing and personal hygiene reveal the importance of these practices in ways that written sources do not (fig. 87). The number and variety of surviving objects associated with taking tea on the one hand and smoking and drinking on the other suggest complex social practices and relationships that transcended "class" lines (figs. 88, 89). Contemporary visual and written references to use of these objects may raise questions of gender distinctions and stereotyping.

Fig. 87. A rare American depiction of a common practice—Peter Manigault and friends toasting one another's success, presumably in Manigault's house after dinner—details various household objects, their placement, and use. George Roupell, Charleston, S.C., ca. 1760, ink and wash on laid paper, H. 10¼" (acc. 63.73).

Fig. 88. *A Society of Patriotic Ladies, at Edenton in North Carolina* captures the importance of tea drinking, a predominantly female ritual in colonial American polite society. The group of ladies, like other groups in the colonies, expressed their political sympathies by signing an agreement to forgo tea (and fabrics) produced in England, thus repudiating English authority in a manner that men did not. Ironically the print was produced and distributed by R. Sayer and J. Bennett of London, in 1775. Mezzotint on laid paper, H. 14¼" (acc. 57.1255).

Fig. 89. The fittings of this chest, called a dressing or shaving table in contemporary design books, indicate that it was made for a man. They include a mirror, two bowls for washing, places for soap dishes and brushes, five bottles (three illustrated), eight small drawers, and a cabinet for storing a chamber pot. Chest: New York City, 1816–25, mahogany and mahogany veneer with secondary woods of white pine and tulip poplar, H. (open) 56¾". Bowls: Andrew Stevenson (w. ca. 1816–30), Cobridge, Staffordshire, transfer-printed pearlware (acc. 65.73a–f). "A. STEVENSON. WARRENTED. STAFFORDSHIRE." is impressed on bottom of lower bowl. Stevenson visited New York City in 1823 in order to develop more business in the United States.

Fig 88

Fig 89

63

Fig 90

Gender roles figured prominently in toys and child-sized furniture, which provided opportunities for children to experiment with and practice adult roles and routines, thereby preparing themselves for later life (fig. 90). Among adults, mourning rings, pictures, and other reminders of mortality expressed grief and helped to prepare individuals for their deaths (figs. 91, 92).

Fig. 90. For the cutouts from a toy theater, males were assigned roles in the military or in farming, while females were given domestic chores that included tending the family garden. "Le Bivoac," France, 1820–30, ink and watercolor on paper, H. of box 1⅛" (Joseph Downs Collection of Manuscripts and Printed Ephemera, Winterthur Library, 74 x 438; gift of Maxine Waldron).

Fig. 91. When Catherine Butler of Hartford, Connecticut, worked a memorial to her brother sometime between 1804 and 1806, symbols of mourning, such as urns and obelisks, weeping willow trees, and mourning figures, as well as their arrangement in a landscape had become highly codified. Mourning art had become a common—almost faddish—way for affluent people to express grief over loss of life. Silk, H. 21" (acc. 58.2876). "CATHERINE BUTLER" is on the reverse-painted glass; "Henry Butler Junr / ob. Sept.br 24th 1804 Æt 19 yrs . . ." is inscribed on the monument.

Fig. 92. This finely engraved silver cup is part of a long tradition of using objects to memorialize the dead. Joseph and Nathaniel Richardson (w. 1777–90), Philadelphia, 1790, silver, H. 2¾" (acc. 77.78; gift of Marshall P. Blankarn). The images of death and time as well as the Latin inscription "so passes worldly glory" follow seventeenth- and early eighteenth-century conventions. "Sic transit Gloria / MUNDI" and "Magdalen Swift died 27th March 1790 = aged 67" engraved on side.

Fig 91

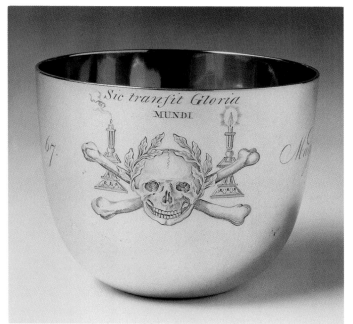

Fig 92

Fig 93

Objects with specific educational or learning functions were indispensable to the process of passing of cultural norms and ideals from person to person and generation to generation. Ownership and use patterns for these objects affirm that education took place in the home as well as in more formal settings. Alphabet exercises taught the rudiments of reading and, in needlework samplers, doubled as instruction in sewing, another educational discipline (fig. 93). Scientific and musical instruments, which number among the finest and most technically sophisticated objects made, exemplify the more extensive education, or "accomplishments," in which "polite," and usually wealthy, men and women were expected to be versed (fig. 94).

Fig. 93. A needlework sampler and horn books with alphabets. Sampler: Abigail Purintun (born ca. 1778), Reading, Mass., 1788, silk on linen, H. 16″ (acc. 63.515). Horn books: England or United States, eighteenth century, horn, L. of longer 4⁷⁄₁₆″ (acc. 55.61.6–7).

Fig. 94. An orrery shows the relative positions and orbits of the planets in their revolution around the sun. The twelve signs of the zodiac and four compass directions are engraved in a brass plate at the top of the base of this orrery along with the inscription, "Constructed by / Joseph C. Hart. / for / Mr. Maguire's Academy. / 1824." New York City, 1824, mahogany, brass, iron, ivory, H. 48¼″ (acc. 70.3).

Fig 94

Messages and Symbols

Objects possess layers of meaning. Investigating their design, construction, uses in the household, and roles in larger social, economic, and cultural networks opens these layers to historical interpretation. In addition, some objects also may be understood through the specific messages or ideas they were meant to convey. Indeed, in some objects, the specific message function is so strong that it obscures everything else about the object. Who can look at George Skinner's large blue-and-white punch bowl and fail to remember his name or wonder who he was (fig. 95)? Likewise, how important were the design subtleties of Robert Livingston's side chair as compared to the visual impact of the elaborate cipher carved into its back (fig. 96)?

Fig. 95. Punch bowl with "GEORGE SKINNER, BOSTON, 1732" painted in large letters around the outside rim. Probably London, England, 1732, tin-glazed earthenware, H. 8⁵⁄₁₆″ (acc. 63.579). Skinner's identity is not known, although men by that name lived in Boston at that time.

Fig. 96. The interwoven initials "RML" carved into the splat are probably those of Robert and Margaret Beekman Livingston, married in 1742, or possibly those of their son Robert and his wife Mary Stevens Livingston, married in 1770. New York City, 1742–70, mahogany, with maple as secondary wood, H. 41½″ (acc. 52.95).

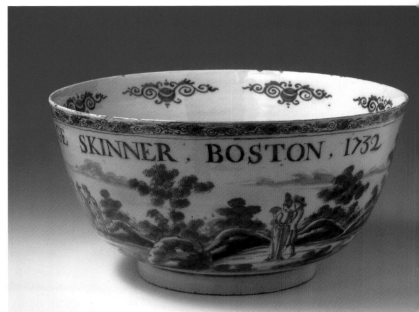

Fig. 95

Fig 96

Fig 97

Initials, dates, inscriptions, insignia, and other special decorations worked into an object at the purchaser's request personalized possessions in revealing ways. Initials typically signify the object's owner, a longstanding practice. They announce "this is mine" (fig. 97). Dates commemorate events, such as marriages or the time of the object's acquisition (fig. 98).

When insignia or symbols referring to social and fraternal organizations are used (with or without identifying initials), the personalized message is "this is who I am" or "this is what I believe in." To the owners of these objects, association of themselves with ideas or groups of people is important. Domestic objects bearing symbols of Freemasonry (a secret fraternal society) or the Order of the Cincinnati (an exclusive fraternity of revolutionary war officers that included George Washington) communicated their owner's power and status through membership in these groups (fig. 99). For those who did not recognize the meaning of these symbols, these objects reinforced the social position and elite status of their owners through exclusion.

Fig. 97. Many of the twenty-five squares in this appliquéd quilt are signed by the women who made them, providing public testimony to both their individual accomplishments and their communal effort. Various makers, Baltimore, Md., 1854, cotton, silk, ink, L. 106½″ (acc. 69.571).

Fig. 98. The owners of this cabinet, made to store valuables, personalized the object by having their initials and "76," for 1676, carved on the door. "B / T+S" probably stands for Thomas and Sarah Buffington of Salem, Massachusetts, who married in 1671, but the significance of 1676 is unknown. Probably Symonds Shop tradition, Salem, Mass., 1676, red oak, maple, black walnut, and red cedar, H. 17¼″ (acc. 58.526).

Fig. 99. The Order of Freemasonry provided its members with social experiences and moral instruction through the performance of secret rituals and ceremonies. Freemasonry also offered prestige and an international network of men with shared values. Some objects with masonic symbols were made for use in lodges, while others for use and display in the home. Plate: China, ca. 1786, hard-paste porcelain, enamel decoration, diam. 9⁹⁄₁₆″ (acc. 63.700.20). Mug: China, 1790–1800, hard-paste porcelain, gilt and enamel decoration, H. 5″ (acc. 56.557). Pitcher: Staffordshire, England, ca. 1820, transfer-printed pearlware, H. 10⅛″ (acc. 83.176).

Fig 98

Fig 99

Fig 100

The likeness of Washington quickly became a meaningful and broadly recognized symbol of patriotism. Gilbert Stuart's striking portrait of Mrs. Perez Morton, a woman admired in her day for her poetry, shows her seated at a table with pen and paper and adjusting her jewelry (fig. 100). The bust of Washington in the background suggests her political beliefs, enlarging the viewer's impression of this wealthy, elegant, and learned woman. Washington's image, like the eagle and related nationalistic symbols (fig. 101), appeared in many forms on many different kinds of objects.

Fig. 100. *Mrs. Perez Morton*, Gilbert Stuart (1755–1828), Philadelphia, 1802–3. Oil on canvas; H. 29½″ (acc. 63.77).

Fig. 101. *American Independence / Declared July 4th. 1776*, a celebratory broadside, uses many commonly recognized symbols in place of words, for example, the hands of unity number thirteen and form a continuous ring. Probably United States, 1776, engraving and watercolor on laid paper, H. 13½″ (acc. 62.190).

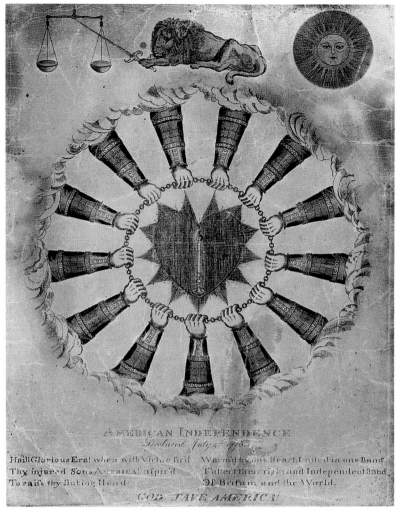

Fig 101

Fig 102

Fig 103

Fig 104

Enthusiasm for Washington reached epic proportions in the years following his death in 1799, culminating in many images that suggest his deification (figs. 102, 103). To a lesser extent, likenesses of other revolutionary war heros and prominent statesmen populated the decorative arts (fig. 104).

Objects also may convey messages and information of varying complexity through pictorial (or iconographic) representations. Some messages are straightforward, others have been obscured by the passage of time and cultural change.

Fig. 102. *Apotheosis of Washington,* a reverse painting on glass, shows angels carrying the late President into the heavens, recreating the image in an 1802 print by John James Barralet of Philadelphia. "SACRED / to the Memory of / WASHINGTON. / OB 11 Dec AD 1799. / Æ t 68." China, 1802–20, oil on glass, H. 26⅝" (acc. 60.570).

Fig. 103. Intense sentiments associated with Washington as a godlike figure are expressed to an extreme on a stoneware jug with the legend "G. WASHINGTON / FOR. EVER" impressed below an applied bust of a bearded man resembling Jesus. Northeastern United States, 1810–40, salt-glazed stoneware, H. 12½" (acc. 61.162).

Fig. 104. Marquis de Lafayette's triumphal return to America in 1824 occasioned numerous celebrations and outpourings of patriotism. The many different kinds of objects honoring him undoubtedly profited their makers and retailers, but for their owners, these trinkets also reaffirmed Lafayette's importance in the formation of the new nation's identity and history. Flask: "LANDING OF GEN. LA FAYETTE / At Castle Garden New York / 16 August 1824," James and Ralph Clews (w. 1819–36), Cobridge, Staffordshire, England, 1824–36, transfer-printed pearlware, H. 6 ¼" (acc. 58.1856). Salt: "LAFAYET.," "B.&.S. / GLASS. / Co.," and "SANDWICH," Boston and Sandwich Glass Company (1825–88), Sandwich, Mass., ca. 1827, lead glass, H. 1⁹⁄₁₆" (acc. 59.3072). Flask: "LAFAYETTE / T.S." and "DE WITT CLINTON / COVENTRY / C–T" Thomas Stebbins, Coventry Glass Works (1813–48), Coventry, Conn., 1824–25, glass, H. 7⅝" (acc. 73.405.2; gift of Mrs. Harry W. Lunger).

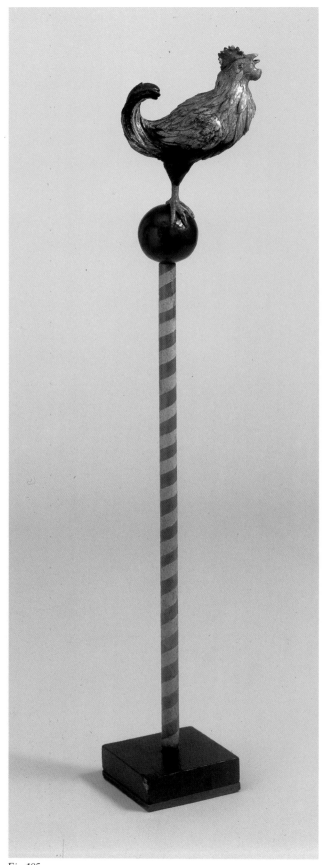

Fig 105

The message imparted by a barber pole and the action embodied in a goldbeater's shop sign still communicate to modern viewers (fig. 105, 106). In contrast, the figures in a needlework picture may appear foreign and somewhat enigmatic to modern eyes. However, eighteenth-century viewers, literate in stories and moral codes of the Bible, would have easily recognized the story of Absalom compacted into a single picture (fig. 107).

Images of historical events and notable personalities on early nineteenth-century domestic objects reflect, on one level, contemporary middle-class interests; on a deeper level, these images suggest a growing awareness of history and, more specifically, the importance of history in American culture as a standard of value. By surrounding themselves with objects that recognized such happenings as Marquis de Lafayette's triumphant return to America in 1824, the growth of canals and railroads, or developments in the arts and sciences, Americans affirmed the historical significance of these events, thereby participating in, if not subtly influencing, the course of history.

Fig. 105. A distinctive striped pole has long signaled a barber, despite changes to the trade of barbering: red and white stripes designated surgical skills; blue signaled hairdressing. The cock atop this particular pole may have identified a specific barber shop. Possibly Pennsylvania, 1800–1870, maple, lead, H. 42⅞" (acc. 59.1803).

Fig. 106. In contrast to complex messages and layers of meaning that certain objects communicated, this shop sign simply announced that a goldbeater, or silversmith, worked there. Probably Boston, nineteenth century, gilded and gessoed wood, H. 20" (acc. 59.1800).

Fig. 107. This needlework picture describes the biblical story of Absalom, who, while riding on a mule, got his head caught in an oak tree: "And [Joab] took three darts in his hand, and thrust them through the heart of Absalom, while he was alive in the midst of the oak. . . . And David sat between the two gates . . . and the king weepeth and mourneth for Absalom" (2 Samuel 18). Salem, Mass., 1760–85, silk, hair, H. 20¼" (acc. 59.1884).

Fig. 106

Fig. 107

Occasionally, a few historical remembrances have been transformed symbolically into embodiments of the past. Chairs that Washington sat in have become memorials, and material remains of witnesses to history were reshaped into icons of history, such as a box made from the elm tree under which William Penn is said to have negotiated land for his colony (fig. 108). The complex cultural processes revealed here evolved into broad-based interests in national and local history by the late nineteenth century. And that sensibility, quaint as it may seem, is a seminal factor in the development of collecting, preserving, and interpreting American decorative arts.

For clarity and convenience, the many objects presented in this essay are interpreted from just one perspective, but each of them can be interpreted from the other five vantage points. Indeed, considering individual objects from two or more perspectives provides fuller understanding and appreciation. If we develop perspectives in addition to the six presented in this essay, we may enrich our understanding of the past even further. Study of the decorative arts seldom yields right and wrong conclusions; instead it enlightens. Learning from objects is an ongoing process that is as intellectually challenging as it is enjoyable and rewarding.

Fig. 108. Affixed to the inside of this box is a picture, signed by Philadelphia antiquarian John Fanning Watson, dated 1823, and inscribed: "The great Elm Tree of Kensington, an emblem of the unbroken Faith of Wm Penn, who held his Treaty with the Indians under its shadow. This box is made of its wood of yr 1810. . . ." A paper tag specifies that the walnut used to edge the box came from trees in front of Independence Hall, and that two stars inlaid in the top came from the house in Santo Domingo where Columbus lived. The box is filled with other relics reportedly collected by Watson, owner of the box. Philadelphia, 1810–23, mahogany, black walnut, elm, and brass, H. (open) 14⅝" (acc. 58.102).

The great Elm Tree ... Kensington, an emblem of the ... with ... Indians ... Faith of Wm Penn, who held his Treat... at its wood, ... 1810. The Walnut ... or its shadow. It stood ... the State House ... shows the last forest tree in Cit... This box is m...

Specimen of Indian Hemp
found 18 feet under ground—
at the shot St. Ricymar Mill.

Fig 108

Photography by George J. Fistrovich
Design by Donald G. Paulhus
The paper is Art Coated
The typeface is Simoncini Garamond
Typeset by Sprintout Corporation, Providence, R.I.
Produced for Winterthur by Fort Church Publishers, Inc.
Little Compton, Rhode Island
Printed in Japan by Dai Nippon